Affirmations for High Achievers™ Volume I: Success

Manifest Big Dreams Through 160 Affirmations and Corresponding Original Piano Compositions

Joseph Kenney

Dedicated to my daughter, Mirabelle; my parents, Chad and Anita; and my brother and sister, Chad Jr. and Jeanna.

Introduction

As I tell everyone who asks me the question, "What made you pursue being a pianist as a career path?" I'll share with you that it originated in sibling rivalry. My brother and sister were exceptionally intelligent and multi-talented. Music was the only place where I outshone them. I was thankful to carve out my own space by dedicating myself to playing the piano.

I started at age 6 and never looked back. By the time I was in high school, I was so committed to practicing that I would get home from school at 2:30 and practice until I was cut off by my sister going to bed at 10:30. What I loved about studying music was how the leaps I was aiming to make as a pianist reflected the work I was doing in every area of my life. I could apply concepts such as direction, intensity, poise, emotional fluctuations, conviction, balance, flow, and many more to both my musical and personal development.

I also had a competitive group of friends. Many of them received considerable recognition for varsity sports and other pursuits. Although I knew my peers generally accepted and appreciated that I had a lot of talent on the piano, on some level, I wanted to prove myself through external confirmation. I entered a piano competition in the 11th grade, fought through anxiety, and prepared diligently. To keep my head and heart clear on the day of the competition, February 4th, 2006, I had an affirming directive as a guiding principle: "Stay in the spirit of the music and keep your mind focused forward."

This "formula" – the revelatory culmination of inner and musical work – led me to victory at the 2006 Marian Garcia Piano Competition.

As an adolescent still developing and as an individual with a fiercely competitive spirit, I started chasing victory. I needed everyone to know I was successful. I was combative and also looking to recreate the high of the victory. I forgot about the inherent beauty of the inner work. Instead of focusing on continued progress through process, I was obsessed with perfection, silencing criticism, and recreating the high of the first-place win. This obsession robbed me of the joy I had experienced up until then, and I lost purpose. Riddled with crippling anxiety, by the time it was time to apply for conservatories, all 12 of the schools I wanted to attend rejected me. In my senior year of high school, I was suicidally depressed. I was diagnosed with bipolar disorder, and by the time I turned 20, I had been hospitalized several times.

I was thankful to be stabilized by medication and my family's support. I went to college locally and received a piano performance degree. At 23, I married and had steady work as a private piano instructor. On paper, these achievements checked all the right boxes, but I still felt unfulfilled.

I was misaligned, heavier than I had ever been, unhappy, and without a sense of inner purpose.

One thing that has always motivated me — maybe it's my competitive side, maybe it's the Philadelphia underdog mentality, or some would say it's because I'm a "Taurus" — was when someone did not believe in me. When my wife left me in 2014, it was a wake-up call. I set and relentlessly pursued incredibly lofty goals to distract me from heartbreak. I broke my huge ambitions into component parts and fully immersed myself in achieving desired results. As part of my process, I focused on tearing down inner barriers preventing me from achieving all I ever wanted for my legacy and love. I had a lot of passive inner negativity to overcome, and I did so through ruthless intentionality in the positive re-wiring of my thoughts.

To hold myself accountable, I gave myself a time limit: I would win a Grammy by age 33.

Along the way, I accomplished a ton, started to carve out my legacy, transformed my mind and body, and reconnected to my soul. I recommitted to inner work, and I fell back in love with the process.

As one who always sought out formulas for progress that I could apply broadly to every song I was practicing or every aspect of my daily life, I realized that when I committed to these personal affirmations — like the one that led me to victory in the formative piano competition — the more external successes aligned with my vision.

I spent eight years creating over 1100 affirmations. I ultimately broke them into several categories of life. The first of which is this inaugural version: Success.

Over this 8 year (and counting) process of compiling affirmations, I accomplished a lot: I won and was nominated for awards as a pianist, composer, and recording artist; became a voting member of the Grammys; ran a successful music festival in support of mental health initiatives; performed with orchestras; embarked on, performed, and managed a DIY national tour with my band; lost 80 pounds; and, strengthened my inner confidence and core relationships.

Moreover, I transformed from a person driven by external accomplishments to a person motivated by process and love. I became a better person as I focused on commitment to inner improvement, and the results then multiplied as my inner glow-up inevitably started to align with tangible results.

I also learned a lot in the journey to becoming, unlearned even more, and maybe most importantly — re-learned things my mind, soul, and body had known intuitively in early adolescence.

My process in writing and embodying each statement in this collection of affirmations can be summarized by "fake it till you make it." I stated qualities about myself I wanted to own as affirmative inner traits I already possessed, and I repeated these affirmations and directives until I stepped into the new realities. I would commit to repeating one affirmation all day. I would literally "walk with it" — while on nature walks or creating music that was inspired by the energy held in each affirmation. There is a QR code for every single affirmation in this book that takes you to correlating original music compositions and performances.

The same existential anxieties that I worked through every day and that led me to document and write my antidotes — the affirmations, theses, and directives that guided me through and onto the other side — were most pervasive when it was time to wind down the collection and complete this book. One book of affirmations blossomed into over multiple volumes and over 1,100 points of growth — which is great in one sense, that inner evolution never stops — but I felt myself avoiding the completion and public release of my work. This is my first book release and the inherent vulnerability in that fact alone summoned doubts of all kinds. Most palpably, the aforementioned nature of the book's "fake it until you make it" statements — by the admission of that definition — would reveal on a public level the depth of my insecurities and limitations I needed to combat. As I am someone who values inner progress, the inner critic was loud on the contention that I was conceding a depth of imperfection which was scary to me.

And in also noting that this 8-year journey marked a "return to myself," the implication that I somehow already knew or practiced these concepts naturally, lost them, and had to regain them, felt like an inner loss that was hard to reconcile. But there is beauty in returning to an inner place that in simpler times your body once knew. And the potential for this book to be a roadmap, blueprint, or way to help even one person positively "back" or "forward" — or both, depending on who utilizes it — takes inner precedence over any and all doubts and resistance to my heart's awareness that this body of work has value.

In the spirit of both "walking the walk" and "talking the talk" — of aligning the statements with my definitive, tangible actions — I release this book and call this volume complete — with the intention that it is received in a way that helps you on your own journey to chase down your goals and evolve mentally, emotionally, spiritually; and that it inspires within you a deeply resonant truth that you are already enough.

As I overlap with all of the following, this book is for:

- [] High achievers in any field
- [] Individuals who struggle with self-doubt
- [] Anyone who has been told directly or otherwise that they are not enough

- [] Those who have felt unworthy of love or only worthy based on others' evaluations of their success
- [] People looking to focus and maximize optimal performance in a sustainable way through meaningful guiding points.
- [] Someone looking for a blueprint for overcoming existential hurdles
- [] Those trying to achieve a mindset conducive to optimal performance while maintaining focus on an inner sense of self that transcends achievements
- [] Recovering perfectionists
- [] Those who want to both leave a legacy of achievement and be a person who grows in the intangibles
- [] One who may need a nudge in the direction of courageous reflection and action
- [] A person struggling with anxiety, depression, and/or bipolar disorder

- Those trying to reconcile with the past in a way that is healthy and forwarding, all while invoking an inner sense of peace
- Persons seeking to get to or return to a place of knowing they are already enough
- Those who need a sign to lean into leading with love, from a new foundation of a positive internal monologue
- And anyone who could benefit from having an adjunctive practical and spiritual tool in a quest to face demons and step into their expansive new reality

My most sincere hope is that if even one of these convictions resonates with you, you will feel emboldened and inspired to make the inner leap that will free the conditions to manifest your life's desires.

Themes and Glossary of Terms

Abundance

This term emphasizes what lies beyond merely giving and receiving to meet expectations and needs, and more-than-safely exceeding your desired level of incoming resources, both tangible and intangible.

Advocacy

Courageous support for yourself and for others

Alignment

When your thoughts, focus, and actions reflect your desired external results

Arrival

The point at which you realize a specific vision

Attune

Inner awareness is an important theme in this book. When I refer to "attuning to an awareness," I am speaking to combining the visualization of your desired effect with an acute sensory awareness of the inner adjustments happening in real time as you shift your mindset.

Aura

What lies within you and makes you a unique person with distinct offerings for the world around you

Authenticity

The unapologetic owning of all that makes you, you

Blessings

Everything you have to be grateful for in your life, whether it is present now or will be in the future

Capability

Confidence in your collection of distinct skills and potential

Champion

To channel your passion into the pursuit of causes you care about

Connection

A vibrational manifestation of empathetic interdependence

Courage

The desire to dream big and live out these dreams, even in a world where there is so much noise and doubt

Deserving

As clarification, I do not believe I am owed anything. I use "deserving" in the context of putting in steady work on yourself, from which the results follow naturally, unsurprisingly, and in that sense, from a place of "deserving" or positive consequence.

Dream

As a verb, to fearlessly wonder and scheme

Elevate

To boldly lift your current state of being into a new challenge, focus, or awareness

Emanate

To exude or become the vibration of a new element of your evolving self

Embody

This is a fancy word that summarizes "fake it until you make it." You embody, or become, the person that could achieve the success of which you dream.

Empathy

Caring about others' feelings. Empathy can be both compassionate when others are struggling amidst your own success, and positive when you are struggling but can feel happy for others in their current victories.

Execute

To carry out the steps involved in making a vision reality

Expansiveness

Expansiveness indicates the state of bringing to life goals bigger than originally anticipated. With inner growth comes inner expansion: There is a certain sense of freedom in knowing that with the right headspace and approach, you can manifest not only the big, scary dreams you have, but also even more.

Flow

When you surrender to the guidance of a directive or affirmation such that your mental and physical state are led by its power

Forward Focus

As opposed to looking backward with a sense of defeat, you maintain an inner compass that looks forward with hope.

Gifts

Talents and abilities we use as tools to make an impact on this world

Inner Light

Used synonymously with aura to mean the spark within you that separates you from everyone else

Inner Work

The prioritization of knowing yourself, and the unending process of evolving to become the best possible version of yourself

Intentions

That which you want to achieve

Investment

While investment is commonly a financial term, I use it to mean the intentional focusing of mental, emotional, and/or spiritual time and energy for self-betterment.

Manifest

To bring goals and dreams to life

Operate

To actively work on yourself in a focused and determined way

Optimal

This book presents experiential formulas that are intended to facilitate a flow state, where you operate at your best or "optimal" level of ability.

Opulence

Used as a synonym for abundance

Poise

Calm, steady, and continuing focus, as anticipatory energy builds in the process of accomplishing a task, goal, or lifelong dream

Release

Letting go of inner hangups and hurdles to pave the way to make space for the successful realization of big goals

Resonate

Physically feeling a positive shift

Safe

A vulnerable theme throughout this collection of affirmations is practicing communication with the body's nervous system as you evolve into newer and newer versions of yourself, with the reminder that although there may be discomfort in the unfamiliar, you are wholly OK to be in a place of growth.

Space

We can be so committed and focused that we can forget to make room, or space, for blessings to happen beyond our wildest goals. Space is both spiritual and tangibly practical.

Spirit

I use spirit to refer to "sacred possibility." It is part-and-parcel of visualization and manifestation, as well as embodying. The spirit, or soul, of what you want to accomplish starts within you.

Synergy

The invisible but ever-present active teamwork of two or more factors

Unknown

This speaks both to the fact that certitude is a fallacy, as well as to having faith in something magical/bigger than us, whether that is a God, the Cosmos, or an unquantifiable energy.

Victory

This has a more personal meaning than emerging triumphant from a confrontation or competition. In this book, a victory encompasses everything from the minutia to the large-scale positive changes in the life-long process of personal development.

Vision

The collection of the biggest dreams and goals you have, and your desire to see them through to fruition

Worthiness

This term hearkens to the battle with imposter syndrome. It is used as a reminder of your inherent uniqueness and value as a human, regardless of others' opinions, or what you do or don't achieve.

Yields

Gains, victories, or results, mainly referring to the byproducts of focus on self-improvement

I invest in the moment, trusting I will arrive.

A process is a series of mistakes, adjustments, and an ultimate realization. Trust the process. Allow the flow of genuine effort to coarse through what is already an immaculate phenomenon. It cannot be improved by false notions of perfection.

I have the strength to align my spiritual energy with that needed to accomplish my goal.

I am resolute as I breathe life into opportunities.

I execute my intentions from a place of relaxation and calm.

I am excited about the possibilities that open when I embrace the energy in giving myself permission to be imperfect.

I have the courage to act with conviction in the face of unknowns.

I act in accordance with my core beliefs and invest in the process, rather than trying to manifest narrow outcomes.

I am poised and ready to strike with optimal energy when the time is right.

I welcome limitless abundance, as I breathe through and release any tensions or doubts.

I manifest patiently — it is all happening.

I am kind to myself on days when I am "unproductive." I practice saying to myself, "Sad days are progress, too." Attributing success to optimal execution, or even a precis sort of happiness, is a limiting and false notion. Processin difficult emotions and allowing myself to be where I am i part of a flow. So, if I can't get myself past a place of urging that "being sad is not a reason to be unproductive, fine. Understandable. I do, though, allow myself to reframe and say, "Days like this are part of the larger process, and my genuine openness and inner honesty regarding the state of my emotions is progress."

I create headspace to allow for the realization of the
intentions I have fostered.

I am thankful to have enough, I am attuned to my dreams and things happen naturally for me.

embrace and am grateful for my wealth, abundance, and recognition.

I am actively grateful for, and celebrating, the success of my colleagues.

I move victoriously forward, with both a focus on the long-game and an openness to immediate results.

On the path to my new destination, I open my heart to new heights, growth, and blessings.

Success attracts successful people; it also attracts jealousy. While I can deploy empathy, I also move on, undistracted in my personal efforts.

I deserve to step into the light of abundance. This light flows through me, and I am healed.

I don't need to prove to anyone that I'm successful.

I am one with the flow of the manifestation of limitless abundance.

I am prepared and poised to flow with the yields of immeasurable success.

I am thankful for who I am; the genuine effort I make to be myself in connecting to and inspiring people is my secret to success.

I am fortunate to lead the life I love.

It's a good day.

I have "it"; the unknown is alive.

I dream big enough to align with a frequency of light that spreads love and happiness.

I dream of huge and lofty goals, and I set expectations with a gentle understanding of the ups and downs that accompany such undertakings.

I believe in myself; I'm doing great and have earned my inner faith.

I bear no responsibility for others' awareness of my successes and inevitable victories. I am unaffected by their surprise when I reach new heights. I operate from a place of love, empathy, and humility.

I have the courage to marry authentic confidence with preparation and humility.

I am unequivocally proud of myself.

Every day, I am changing the world with my gifts.

I am free as I resonate with a deep understanding that I deserve my successes.

I combine a strong passion for imparting meaningful change with a deep sense of relaxation and of knowing in my soul everything is okay.

I calmly embrace uncertainty and leverage optionality: Endless pathways to the realization of meaningful goals exist.

Courageous hope fuels my vision.

I am gracious as I receive recognition for my hard work and success.

An abundant energy accumulates in the consistency of elevated micro-actions: I give myself credit for, and recognize the momentum in, small changes that add to a synergistic whole. I have faith that my efforts yield desirable results.

am the best; I do not need to be the best; my objective is to have fun and be my best.

The act is the way. Go forth trusting the larger vision, one act at a time.

Stick to the plan; it's working.

I trust the impact I am having.

My legacy endures through the people I inspire and the people they in turn inspire.

I can simultaneously be grateful for my abundance and embrace that I have earned my current level of success and the future wins I will continue to see.

Even in periods when I am physically silent, I trust the results that unfold. I am patient in my awareness of the spiritual dynamism in silence.

I am proud of my continuous inner work, and I have patience in knowing it will lead to success that aligns with my level of commitment.

I am using my gifts in meaningful and plentiful ways.

I'm thankful for the opportunities in the unknown, and I trust myself to be in a space of empowered waiting.

I embrace serendipitous, good things.

Celebrating in the moment is critical to developing the inner peace I will draw from when I face challenges in the future.

I am grateful when others want to invest in my vision. At the same time, I honor my awareness of the intrinsic worthiness and light I possess.

I have a sense of peace and trust in the realization of inevitable harmony, and I manage the unexpected ways in which a vision is realized and comes together.

As I optimally execute my vision for the future, I relax and release expectations of specific outcomes, which clears the way for abundant returns.

I trust in the productiveness of joyfully assessing the big picture.

I am optimistic that everything will work out.

I am recharged as I let myself dream without limits or worries.

I am open to and thankful for whatever "wins" come my way.

I release all need for external proof of, or accolades for, my worth, as I enjoy continued happiness and success.

I am more than my accomplishments.

I am thankful to make a meaningful difference through the expansive artistic realization of my bold vision.

I courageously embrace how capable I am.

I commit to the process so intensely that the goal is an afterthought: The process is the dream.

Everything is falling into place — and I'm ready to embrace that.

I enthusiastically embrace the premise that I am amazing
I can remain humble and focused while simultaneously
embracing the awareness that I am inherently incredible

The collection of my broken pieces is one big victory story.

I deserve the inner abundance that I have created and have consequently invited to opulently multiply.

No amount of intelligence nor planning can substitute for taking time to surrender to the flow of marvel and wonder.

I let go of what I once revered as if they were legends and lore, and become who I am.

I have the patience to practice.

I am resilient. I have faith in my ability to access my inner power and advocate for what matters most.

I am intelligent and my accomplishments are plentiful.

I forge my path to victory through inner harmony.

I have the poise to continue to be conviction-driven, as abundant yields provide a monumental and welcome exhale.

I am thankful for the respect I've earned from myself and others, and I have the right to protect my energy from the spirit of jealousy.

All will manifest.

I take pride in the credibility I've established. My awareness of the substantial good I've done empowers m to advocate for myself and others.

I give myself space to experience joy.

I provide value in the resource of my accessibility.

I achieve my potential by looking within.

I release the need for confirmation of my worthiness. Thi results in attraction and arrival, and can be applied as a meditation across all work and personal goals.

elevate the intersection of awareness of being deserving of a specific goal, and releasing the need for the actualization of one specific external outcome.

I celebrate my resounding life victories and continue to joyfully ascend, as I remain unmoved by external misperceptions.

I remain open to the process of trying and calibrating my next attempt, according to the results of my efforts.

I am a constant champion of myself.

I have, and have always possessed, full worthiness from within.

I am safe to celebrate my victories.

I am enlivened by an intuitive awareness of my talents.

I take time for the precise execution of my intentions.

I am safe to prioritize inner victories and to receive the plentiful yields of that inner focus.

I am safe to be humble; I am safe to be discovered; I am safe to be myself; I am safe to be playful as I optimally shine.

I have patience and a sense of inner calm, as the universe aligns to reflect the dreams I have worked toward.

a

I respect and nurture my limitlessness by intentionally setting boundaries. I do not need to be everything to everyone. I can say "no." These acts honor the toll my success and active goodness can have on my mind, body, and spirit.

I am safe to expect the best in me, even when others do not believe in me or do not understand my motivation.

I resolve to know myself, even when things go well.

I trust everything will work out, as I stay fearlessly committed to organization and timeliness.

I am steady. I am un-anxious. I possess a spirit of inner peace. I am limitlessly capable and do not need to prove anything. I have already won.

I am undistracted and am without worry, as I allow others to underestimate me.

I have the right to set boundaries for both positive and negative feedback. I decide how much access I give others to engage with me directly about their perceptions of my life.

have the grace to be kind as I go on my way. Even when people have not seen where I have been or where I am going, I remain poised in the resolute calm of knowing where I am headed and that I will arrive.

I have and exercise the right to be happy, independent of
my accomplishments.

I am at peace knowing my dreams have come true and new blessings are being actualized, from my foundation of the inner certainty that I am fundamentally abundant and sufficient.

I act in alignment with the pride I have in my convictions. Therefore, I am my own P.R. person, approaching every interaction with fearless authenticity.

I am thankful for the expansiveness I can enjoy by unequivocally cheering on others to ascend to their highest possible heights, even when they achieve a goal I strive toward. I root for others wholeheartedly, and have empathy for anyone who has not yet reached a place where they can genuinely cheer on others.

I am safe to be here — I am safe to focus — I am safe to do
my best.

I stay poised and trust myself, as I execute with intuitive awareness of all I am capable of doing.

My new foundation transcends outcomes.

As I am peacefully led by allowing a spirit light to shine through my unwavering creation process, I know I am enough.

As I embark on my journey to realize everything I dream of, I can heal my inner child and return to the intuitive awareness that I have always had an inner bounty bigger than my external pursuits could ever reveal.

I understand the solemnity of continuing to improve, so I can model joyously trying and failing at new things to those I love and mentor. I know that "failing" is relative, a process, and a necessity for ultimate success.

I demonstrate composed fearlessness and recognize that I need to feel safe, within myself, to fail in a healthy and steady way.

I am open to all possibilities of maximum splendor.

I embrace the blessings of all avenues to expansion, while staying true to my convictions.

I am the sole arbiter of my inner worth.

I am steady as I emanate opulent inner confidence and worthiness.

I proclaim victory within.

I maintain steadiness as I embrace inner and outer yields with gratitude.

I keep going.

I am appreciative of the inspiration provided by those I love and admire.

I honor the sacredness of opportunity.

I am secure in the awareness of the depth of all I deserve.

I celebrate inner strength, by giving myself grace when I triumph and showing compassion for others' setbacks.

I give myself credit and gratitude: My body of work speaks for itself.

celebrate my incremental progress, just as I celebrate the big leaps.

I am proud, happy, and limitless as I reflect on the depth execution, and success of my vision.

As I let the vision breathe, I am safe to take breaks and peacefully contemplate.

I surrender to the expansiveness of relaxation as a form of inner activation.

I am proud of the fruits of my high expectations, as I begin incorporating elements of restfulness.

I expand my operational state of poise: I know what need
to be done and I get it done.

I encourage others to grow into their best selves.

I find the home in my soul, as my dreams come true.

I trust the horizon and allow myself to flourish.

I am independent in the estimation of my progress.

I declare victory in my story, without ascribing a villain.

I build on my fundamental sufficiency with a love of the process and a commitment to consistency.

I let the unknowns enhance the bounty of my work.

To balance my intense focus on leveling up, I rest in appreciation of all I have accomplished.

I access my inner truth without encumbrance: I have realized alignment in manifestation.

I live and breathe in exultant reprieve: I've made it.

I am a victorious spirit in a victorious reality.

I am connected to, and embody, the energy of the effect I wish to impart.

I am loving and happy in my productivity, as I see my dreams come true. I display rebellious indifference to animosity, doubt, and dissent.

I am intentionally indifferent to those who choose not to see, love, acknowledge, or believe in me.

I accept the blessings I have prayed and worked for, as I lift the fallacy that I need to do more or be more to receive abundantly.

I win with elegance; my convincing, loving victories heal hearts and mend minds.

I am attuned to the depth of my inner magic, an end unto itself.

I am safe to see the ways in which things have worked out

I hone a Herculean disinterest in noise.

I have an amazing life, as I build from a healthy and focused place.

With self-compassion, I learn to take my time as I lift the burden of my intensity toward all I want to accomplish.

I am well-positioned to manage bountiful returns with ease and grace, as I detach from the pressure of threading the needle on a restrictive vision.

I commit to finding my zone, allowing all else to take care of itself.

I remove all doubt.

I address feedback and stimulus without abruptly changing course.

I troubleshoot my next steps, as I break free from backtracking and attacks on my inner peace.

I stick with the power of love and my vision, as I am un-swept by the pull of competition.

I empower a rebellious peace of mind as I disregard external narratives.

I allow for a continuity of inner peace, while exhibiting a willingness to live outside my comfort zone; I invite ebb and flow as I detach from fear.

I stay in the spirit of the music, as I keep my mind focused forward.

About The Author

Joe Kenney is an award-winning pianist, recording artist, and composer, and a voting member of the Grammys. He provides music instruction, manages artists, and advocates for mental health awareness. Joe hails from the Greater Philadelphia Area.

Joe has released six albums and countless collaborations. Musically, these productions span multiple genres. They reflect a cohesive blend of classical, jazz, rock, soul, and hip-hop elements. Joe has garnered praise for both his original compositions and cover arrangements.

His debut solo piano album, Afflictions and Remedies (2015) received local airplay. It was also praised as a "painting of a piano at work" by Meredith Hairston, who put the album in rotation at WJSU in Jackson, MS.

In 2016, Joe went to work on an album of jazz and classical-inspired arrangements of alternative rock and Top 40 hits. Released in February 2016 and titled *1.5*, the album was recognized on broadcast radio 104.5 Philadelphia and featured on *iHeartRadio*. DJ Wendy Rollins characterized Joe's cover of the Twenty One Pilots' song *Stressed Out* as "perfection" and went on to applaud him for "re-imagining songs in a completely different format."

Following the success of his first two solo piano albums, Joe expanded by adding new formats to his musical output. Working with a full band, he homed in on a jazz fusion sound while retaining the classically informed harmonies from his first two albums. An EP of three singles was released in 2017, which became the foundation and inspiration for the 2020 album *Forth*.

In March 2018, Joe released *2.5*, his third full studio album in as many years. Showcasing multiple styles and varying instrumentation, *2.5* features distinctively energized reinterpretations of eight alternative rock hits. The first half of the album features two full-group instrumental tracks and two vocal arrangements. The second half of the album features solo piano re-imaginings of four additional songs. Two tracks from the project were placed on the official iHeartRadio "Instrumental Pop Covers" playlist.

In August 2018, Joe made waves with his debut orchestral performance. The Chester County Pops premiered his original work *Zera* alongside a performance of Chopin's *Andante Spianato et Grande Polonaise Brillante*.

In 2019, Kenney started recording his fourth album. His biggest undertaking to this point, *Forth* would feature six highly decorated vocal artists from the Philadelphia area on a ten-track original album. The music is geared to markets that cross multiple musical styles. The first single *Another Side (Ft. Joy Ike)*, released on May 8th, 2020, was premiered by Neon Music (UK) and earned a glowing review. The track was also featured on *The Key/WXPN*, and popular radio personality Helen Leicht selected it as the Philly Local Pick. The next two releases, *All's Not Lost (Ft.*

Laura Lizcano), and *Gone (Ft Aaron Parnell Brown)*, also garnered spectacular reviews.

On October 23rd, 2020, the full album – *Forth* – was released to all platforms. It won a Bronze Medal in the Global Music Awards and has been featured on over eighty-five Radio Stations in the U.S. and Canada.

After pushing the tour in support of the album back due to the Covid pandemic, Kenney continued to work on more material and collaborations with new artists for future releases.

During this time, Joe also recorded an entirely new solo piano project, his fifth studio album, titled *Reflections on Inner Transformation.* The music features explorations and meditations on points of personal growth Kenney sought to develop. The spirit of each point is captured in sound.

Four singles from the album were released in 2021, and popular music blogs such as *Music Dances When You Sleep* and *MainlyPiano* featured the music.

A year after the release of *Forth,* in October 2021, Joe Kenney Band brought the *Forth Tour* to fruition. The four-piece band performed concerts for enthusiastic crowds in Cleveland, OH; Louisville, KY; Birmingham, AL; New York, NY; Wayne, PA; and Wilmington, DE.

After the momentum of the group's first tour together, Joe and his band maintained an impressively active schedule in 2022, with debuts at World Cafe Live, TIME, Heritage, SOUTH Jazz Club, City Winery, Kennett Brewing

Company Jazz Fest, and a weekly residency at Root Down Brewing Company in Phoenixville.

Root Down Brewing Co. collaborated with Joe on a beer that commemorates and bears the same name as the *Reflections on Inner Transformation* album. Released in May 2022, "Reflections" debuted at 15 on the Zone Music Reporter charts. The album was also minted as an NFT project, with Joe partnering with his *The Proper Hustlers* bandmate and cryptocurrency guru Chris Fox.

December 2022 saw the release of *Prevailing*, a classical/cinematic collaboration between Joe and fellow West Chester University alumna, violinist Hope Linton. *Prevailing* debuted at #2 on the One World Music Radio Charts, and the album received an overwhelmingly positive response, with a flurry of reviews celebrating the composition and the record.

New music, eclectic collaborations, a bevy of shows, and prolific releases continued as the theme of 2023. Joe produced nine studio releases and reached over 1 million total Spotify plays. Between his six bands and solo efforts, he performed in over 125 shows. At the same time, Joe focused on content creation online, amassing over 1,000 subscribers on YouTube, and creating a multitude of symphonic works ready to be arranged for full orchestra.

In 2024, Joe teamed up with Katie Butler and Candice Johnson-Lindsay to create, organize, and curate the inaugural Harmonic Hope & Healing Festival, which brought awareness to music therapy and mental health initiatives.

HHH Fest took place on 5/5/24 in Philadelphia and featured a star-studded six-band lineup, a sound healing space, vendors, and practitioner demonstrations.

www.ingramcontent.com/pod-product-compliance
Lightning Source LLC
Chambersburg PA
CBHW021632120626
46545CB00002B/502